CIVIL WARRIOR

The Extraordinary Life and Complete Poetical
Works of James Graham,
First Marquis of Montrose
Warrior and Poet
1612–1650

James Graham, First Marquis of Montrose.
Engraved by W. Holl from the painting by Gerard van Honthorst.

CIVIL WARRIOR

The Extraordinary Life and Complete Poetical
Works of James Graham,
First Marquis of Montrose
Warrior and Poet
1612–1650

Edited with a commentary by
ROBIN BELL

Luath Press Limited

EDINBURGH

www.luath.co.uk

First Published 2002

The paper used in this book is recyclable. It is made from low
chlorine pulps produced in a low energy, low emission manner from
renewable forests.

The publisher acknowledges subsidy from

 Scottish **Arts** Council

towards the publication of this volume.

Printed and bound by
Cromwell Press, Trowbridge

Designed by Tom Bee

Typeset in 10.5 Quadraat by S. Fairgrieve

CONTENTS

INTRODUCTION

He either fears his fate too much
Or his deserts are small
That puts it not unto the touch
To win or lose it all.

FOUR CENTURIES AFTER they were written, these lines are still quoted whenever someone needs to summon up the courage to do the right thing, rather than submit to the easy option.

Like many familiar quotations, The Bible or Shakespeare is often assumed to be the source. In fact, the man who wrote these words, James Graham, First Marquis of Montrose (1612 – 1650) was conceived in the year that the standard King James Authorised Version of The Bible was first published and Shakespeare's *Tempest* was first produced. His short life was spent at the epicentre of the storm over religio-cultural independence which plunged Britain into civil war.

Montrose lived his life by his own maxim *To win or lose it all*. The motto on his battle standard was *Nil Medium*. He was both Scotland's great cavalier poet and a brilliant military strategist who held the highest office in the land, Lieutenant Governor of Scotland, for six years. Admired and hated for his unswerving loyalty and integrity in the face of the slithery politics of Puritan hypocrisy, he was executed in Edinburgh at the age of thirty-seven.

As a literary figure, he was held in great esteem by contemporaries such as Drummond of Hawthornden. Across the centuries, he has struck a chord with writers of very different political temperaments. Voltaire, in his *Essaie sur l'Histoire Generale* praises both the nobility and the art of *Let Them Bestow on Every Airth a Limb*, written by Montrose on the eve of his execution.

In an era which produced many men of dual talents, Bacon, Surrey, Milton, Marvell, Rochester and others divided their work between their literary careers and service to their respective heads of state. Only Sir Walter Raleigh, however, comes close to matching Montrose in breadth of accomplishment.

Montrose lived at a time when Scottish constitutional independence was a central issue and when public opinion was generally against the royal family. Slippery deals, cynical spin, smug grandees and greedy newcomers were rife. As Scotland began to fragment under the burden of separate ambitions of a host of political opportunists, Montrose fought to maintain national stability.

Montrose's poems are not the weasel words of a desk-bound politician. They are the passionate affirmations of a man of action. His enemies feared his compelling honesty as much as his brilliant military victories. After he was betrayed and captured in 1650, a book containing one of his poems was hung round his neck as he was executed. That is how much these poems meant in his own time. All that survive are printed here.

Because Montrose never wrote an autobiography, this book is designed to give readers access to what survives of his most intimate writing, placed in the context of his turbulent times. It is simply a chance to let the man speak for himself.

Robin Bell
October 2002

Montrose's battle standard.
Nil Medium: No Middle Way.

I

The Montrose burial ground at Aberuthven, Perthshire.
Engraved by W. Brown from the painting by William Bell Scott.

EARLY YEARS

JAMES GRAHAM was born in 1612 into one of Scotland's most politically active families with lands ranging across central Scotland and further north around Montrose. Sir John de Graham fought alongside William Wallace and was killed at the Battle of Falkirk in 1298. Sir David Graham was an ally of Robert Bruce. The family was raised to the peerage in 1445 and thereafter maintained a loyalty to the Stewart dynasty greater than these capricious Scottish monarchs deserved. Grahams supported James II against the mighty house of Douglas. Grahams stood by James III in the face of a rebellion of nobles.

James IV made Montrose into an earldom in 1503, only to die alongside the First Earl at the Battle of Flodden. The Second Earl was the only Scottish noble to attend the first mass in Scotland of the young Mary, Queen of Scots. The Third Earl was a protestant reformer, becoming Viceroy of Scotland when James VI headed south to take up the throne of England. The Fourth Earl was President of Charles I's Privy Council. When he died on 12 November 1626, his fourteen year old son, James inherited the title. At his birth it was rumoured that witches had foretold this boy 'would trouble all Scotland'. They were right.

When Montrose's father was buried in the Graham mausoleum in the Perthshire village of Aberuthven, the young Earl led his kinsmen in a funeral feast at nearby Kincardine Castle that was to last six weeks. Huge quantities of venison, wildfowl and other game from the Graham estates in the parish of Auchterarder and elsewhere were set beside sides of beef and lamb and washed down with gallons of ale and fine wines. Throughout his life, Montrose was rich in land and poor in ready cash. His generosity was deep. His purse was not. He was forced to mortgage properties to finance a lifestyle fitting for the national role all assumed he would play.

A young noble was expected to learn the arts of war, the arts of the table and the arts of scholarship, usually in that order. Two months after his father's death Montrose went to St. Andrews University to hone these skills. He did so with some distinction.

He won the silver arrow for archery in 1628 and 1629. This was no trivial local competition. In 1623, the silver arrow was won by the future Marquis of Argyll, who was to become Montrose implacable enemy. In 1624, it was won by the future Earl of Morton, Argyll's cousin. In 1625 it was won by David Leslie who became the only general to defeat Montrose in battle. In 1626 it was won by Lord Elcho who fled from Montrose at the Battle of Tibbermore.

Montrose was a good all-round sportsman. He was a skilled horseman and swordsman and inherited his father's fondness for golf. He also loved music, particularly the bagpipes, and was generous in paying pipers and fiddlers. His main scholarly interest was military and political history. One of his favourite books was Walter Raleigh's *History of the World*, which he carried in his personal baggage to St. Andrews. Raleigh's romantic breadth of vision and heroic personal achievements inspired the young Montrose. He also read widely in the classics and became fascinated by Alexander the Great.

Montrose's earliest recorded poems are written on the flyleaves of his books. In his copy of Lucan's epic poem 'Pharsalia', he notes that Macedo (Alexander the Great) always carried a copy of Homer's works. Montrose says he prefers Lucan, then soars off into imagining what great deeds he might achieve himself if the Fates give him the chance to prove himself. It is a combination of callow arrogance and prescient sense of his potential.

As Macedo his Homer, I'll thee still
Lucan, esteem as my most precious gem;
And though my fortune second not my will,
That I may witness to the world the same,
Yet if she would but smile ev'n so on me,
My mind desires as his and soars as he.

In his copy of Quintus Curtius's romantic history of Alexander the Great, son of Philip of Macedon, Montrose idealises his hero as a model for achieving fame and glory for himself, 'an eternal name'.

As Philip's noble son did still disdain
All but the dear applause of merited fame
And nothing harboured in that lofty brain
But how to conquer an eternal name;
So great attempts, heroic ventures shall
Advance my fortune or renown my fall.

His reading of mediaeval crusading tales reinforced his vision of himself as a man of honour, ready to give his life for God and King. At this early stage of his life, he was aware that he had achieved nothing yet on the national political scene, but could still have a noble code of conduct as high as anyone's. On the flyleaf of his copy of Caesar's *Commentaries*, he wrote,

Though Caesar's paragon I cannot be,
Yet shall I soar in thoughts as high as he.

By the time Montrose left St. Andrews in 1629, he was a slim figure of medium height and commanding presence. His unfailing courtesy and generosity made him popular among commoners, but his fierce sense of responsibility could turn into biting sarcasm directed at any of his peers who failed to live up to what he saw as their patrician duty. It was a trait that would earn him loyal respect and bitter enmity.

II

Montrose at the time of his marriage. Aged seventeen.

Engraved by R. Bell from the painting by George Jamesone.

MARRIAGE AND TRAVELS

He was of a middle stature and most exquisitely proportioned limbs; his hair of a light chestnut; his complexion betwixt pale and ruddy; his eye most penetrating though inclining to grey; his nose aquiline...

As he was strong of body and limbs, so he was most agile, which made him excel most of others in those exercises where these two are required. In riding the great horse and making use of his arms he came short of none. I never heard much of his delight in dancing though his countenance and his other bodily endowments were equally fitting the court as the camp...

He made it his business to pick up the best of their (foreign scholars) qualities necessary for a person of honour. Having rendered himself perfect in the academics his next delight was to improve his intellectuals, which he did by allotting a proportional time to reading and conversing with learned men; yet still so that he used his exercise as he might not forget it. He studied as much of the mathematics as is required for a soldier. But his great study was to read men and the actions of great men...

Thus he spent three years in France and Italy: and would have surveyed the wonders of the east, if his domestic affairs had not obliged his return.

Thomas Sydserf, son of the Bishop of Galloway and one of
Montrose's travelling companions in Europe.

I T WAS, and bizarrely still is, a peer's duty to produce a male heir as quickly as possible. By the summer of 1629, Montrose had spent over two years at St. Andrews University though he had not yet reached the age of seventeen. It was time for him to leave and marry.

Montrose's mother had died when he was only six, but his five sisters meant that he had no lack of female family presence while he was growing up. Montrose had no brothers until, probably after his mother's death, his father sired an illegitimate son, Harry, who was to become Montrose's close friend and lieutenant.

Montrose's mother was Margaret Ruthven, daughter of the Earl of Gowrie whose family was deeply entangled in Scotland's violent past. Her father was executed for conspiracy and her two brothers had been killed at Huntingtower then posthumously accused by James VI of conspiracy. The Gowries were alleged to use witchcraft against their enemies and Montrose's mother was rumoured to have consulted witches after his birth. Witches, their spells and fortune-telling were taken seriously in Montrose's day. Outside Dunning, two miles from the Graham Mausoleum in Aberuthven, stands the cross of Maggy Wall who was burned for witchcraft in 1657.

Montrose inherited neither his mother's supposed taste for witchcraft nor his father's very real addiction to the tobacco which damaged his health. What he and his sisters did inherit from their mother was an attraction to intellectual pursuits at the highest level. Lilias, his eldest sister, married Sir John Colquhoun of Luss, an urbane scholar who had travelled widely in Europe. Montrose's second sister, Margaret, married Archibald Napier of Merchiston, son of the great Scottish mathematician.

Archie Napier was a generous spirited man of great breadth of vision, close enough to the centre of politics to give sceptical guidance in the ways of Scottish government. He remained a lifelong ally of the young Montrose whose circle now included poets like William Drummond of Hawthornden who was later to write 'The Golden Age is returned' when Montrose gave him protection to publish previously suppressed work.

Montrose thrived in the lively company of his brothers in

law's households. We do not know much about his early romantic attachments, except that in later life, when his personal papers were seized by his enemies, hoping to find state secrets, they only discovered bundles of letters 'flourished with Arcadian compliments' which young ladies had sent to him. It appears that he enjoyed women and, true to his gallant character, enjoyed them discreetly.

In his poem In Praise of Women, Montrose does not show any of the unrequited lover's anguish or tortuous metaphysical conceits that were popular at the time. Instead, he conventionally calls man a superior being and 'that poor creature', made out of Adam's spare rib, an even more superior one. He then compliments women bluntly by calling them beautiful flowers at the end of a male 'stubborn stalk' and says he has no time for those who fail to make love enthusiastically or simply say no. To twenty first century readers, his cavalier frank attitude to women is perhaps more shocking than The Earl of Rochester's obscene rhyming extravaganzas.

IN PRAISE OF WOMEN.

When heaven's great Jove had made the world's
round frame,
Earth, water air and fire; above the same,
The ruling orbs, the planets, spheres and all
The lesser creatures, in the earth's vast ball:
But, as a curious alchemist still draws
From grosser metals finer and from those
Extracts another, and from that again
Another that doth far excel the same,
So framed he man of elements combined

T' excel that substance whence he was refined;
But that poor creature, drawn from his breast
Excelleth him, as he excelled the rest;
Or as a stubborn stalk, whereon there grows
A dainty Lilly or a fragrant Rose,
The stalk may boast and set its virtues forth,
But take away the flow'r, where is its worth?

    But yet, fair ladies, you must know
    Howbeit I do adore you so;
    Reciprocal your flames must prove,
    Or my ambition scorns to love.
    A noble soul doth still abhor
    To strike but where it's conqueror.

When it came to finding a wife, Montrose, as a highly eligible young Earl might have been expected to choose the eldest daughter of a senior noble house. Instead, in November 1629, a few months after leaving St. Andrews University, he married Magdalen Carnegie who was the closest thing to the girl next door. Magdalen was the sixth daughter of a new peer, Lord Kinnaird, whose estate lay close to Montrose's own lands of Auld Montrose. Kinnaird was an able and ambitious administrator who married off all of his daughters to more senior nobility and was himself eventually elevated to the Earldom of Southesk.

No account survives of Montrose's wedding at the parish church of Kinnaird. One can only hope that it was as enjoyable an affair as his father's funeral. Along with Magdalen, Montrose received a dowry of £40,000 which went some way towards restoring his depleted finances.

For the next three years Montrose lived mainly at Kinnaird. It was the most tranquil phase of his adult life. His two eldest sons, John and James, were born and he led a life blending agreeable sport with further serious reading.

As for that hopeful youth, the young Lord Graham,
James, Earl of Montrose, whose war-like name
Sprung from redoubted worth, made manhood try
Their matchless deeds in unmatched chivalry,

I do bequeath him to thy gracious love,
Whose noble stock did ever faithful prove
To thine old-aged ancestors; and my bounds
Were often freed from thraldom by their wounds,
Leaving their root, the stamp of fidele truth,
To be inherent in this noble youth,

Whose hearts, whose hands, whose swords, whose deeds, whose fame,
Made Mars for valour, canonise the Graham.

William Lithgow. Scotland's Welcome to her Native Son and Sovereign Lord, King Charles I. 1633.

The tranquillity of Montrose's own marriage was contrasted in 1631 by the collapse of his oldest sister Lilias's marriage, made all the more dramatic when her husband eloped with her younger sister, Katherine. Rumours flew of drugged love philtres and necromancy. The scandal was still the talk of Scottish society when Montrose reached the age of twenty-one and, his majority attained, set off on a tour of Europe.

We do not know the precise route Montrose took, nor how long he stayed in each place during the time he spent in France, Italy and Germany from 1633 to 1636. It had already become fashionable for a young man to broaden his horizons by taking a Grand Tour of Europe. Remarkably, this was still the case while the Thirty Years War (1618–48) was raging. It was possible to travel widely if one had some common sense and was fairly up to date with troop movements. There were plenty of Scottish professional soldiers serving in the various armies engaged in the Thirty Years War and, with Montrose's good family connections, it is likely that he had fairly good intelligence of which destinations were desirable at any given time.

Like any man of rank, he travelled with servants and companions. It was not merely a case of sight-seeing and cultural dabbling. He studied the arts of war at Angers, where the vast castle was an example of state-of-the-art military fortification.

He acquired a knowledge of the campaign strategies and tactics used by the great Gustavus Adolphus of Sweden who was killed in 1633. Montrose's taste for hard fact and sound procedure was offset by a need to delve into the unknowable. His fascination with destiny caused him, according to one of his travelling companions, Basil Fielding (the future Lord Denbigh), to consult several astrologers while they were in France.

During his travels he acquired a little French bible which is now at Innerpeffray Library, not far from where he grew up near Auchterarder. In its flyleaves are Latin and Italian mottos which appealed to his code of honour.

King Charles I.
Engraved by T. W. Knight from the painting by VanDyck.

La Vita passa, la morte viene; Beato colui chi havra fatto bene

(Life passes, death comes; Blessed is the man who has done right)

Ardito e presto

(Passionate and swift)

Aut solvam, aut diruam

(I shall either set it free or destroy it)

Pro jocundis, aptissima quoque Deus dat

(For our delight, God gives what suits us best)

The last can be more cuttingly translated as: For amusement, God gives us what we deserve. Montrose was quick-witted in his wordplay as in his swordplay.

Three years was a long time for a young husband to be away from his wife and children. We do not know how he and Magdalen felt about one another in this period, but he wrote a poem, possibly during these travels, which talks about desire and absence, 'T'abound yet have no treasure'. He says, in his usual blunt way, 'Flames not maintained soon faileth' but characteristically refuses to despair and hopes 'my star will change her air'. It would be unwise to interpret too much precise biographical detail from his words but it shows that aspect of Montrose and all the Grahams that will not be deflected from duty, even if affection and support are absent, but is much more at ease if just one person shows a 'perfect sympathy in love'.

PERFECT SYMPATHY IN LOVE.

There's nothing in this world can prove
So true and real pleasure
As perfect sympathy in love,
Which is a real treasure.

The purest strain of perfect love,
In virtue's dye and season,
Is that which influence doth move,
And doth convince our reason.

Designs attend, desires give place;
Hope had, no more availeth;
The cause removed, the effect doth cease;
Flames not maintained soon faileth.

The conquest then of richest hearts,
Well lodg'd and trimmed by nature,
Is that which true content imparts,
Where worth is joined with feature.

Fill'd with sweet hope then must I still
Love what's to be admired;
When frowning aspects cross the will,
Desires are more endeared.

Unhappy then unhappy I,

To joy in tragic pleasure,

And in so dear and desperate way

T'abound yet have no treasure.

Yet will I not of fate despair;

Time oft in end relieveth;

But hope my star will change her air

And joy where now she grieveth.

It was time for Montrose to come home, not just to see his family, but to become directly involved in the affairs of Scotland as family expectation and his own sense of duty dictated.

First he had to be presented at court in London, where the Stewart dynasty had established themselves in preference to Edinburgh after the Union of the Crowns of Scotland and England in 1603. Montrose's father has served King Charles I as President of The Privy Council, and it was reasonable to expect the king to welcome the young Lord Montrose to the court.

All courts have their rituals. To be presented to Charles I, Montrose had to be sponsored by a senior peer. Montrose asked the Marquis of Hamilton to be his sponsor. We do not know why. Perhaps it was in part because Hamilton was the brother in law of Montrose's recent travelling companion Denbigh. The Hamiltons were themselves a senior branch of the Stewarts, but the current Marquis was a nervous schemer and viewed the confident young Montrose as a potentially dangerous rival for the King's favours. We do not know what Hamilton said to Charles I about Montrose, but the formal presentation in 1636 was a disaster. In front of a large audience, the king merely extended his hand to be kissed and then turned coldly away. Montrose was shocked and disappointed. The snub did not make him any

James,
First Duke of Hamilton.

Engraved by W. Linton.

the less loyal to the king, but it was a rude introduction to the slippery ways of the court.

Montrose quickly sized up Hamilton and lampooned him in a poem. Hamilton liked to pose as a military expert, having served under Gustavus Adolphus, though that great general had never trusted him in the realities of front line duty. Montrose seized upon a ludicrous incident to show exactly what level of military combat Hamilton was fit for.

Some Lines on the Killing of the Earl of Newcastle's Son's Dog, by the Marquess Hamilton, in the Queen's Garden at York.

Here lies a dog, whose qualities did plead
Such fatal end from a renowned Blade;
And blame him not, though he succumbed now,
For Hercules could not combat against two;
For while he on his foe revenge did take,
He manfully was stabbed behind his back.
    Then say, to eternise the cur that's gone,
    He fleshed the maiden sword of Hamilton.

III

THE NATION DIVIDES

We declare before God and men, that we have no intention nor desire to attempt anything that may turn to the dishonour of God, or to the diminution of the king's greatness and authority; but, on the contrary, we promise and swear, that we shall to the uttermost of our power, with our means and lives, stand to the defence of our dread sovereign the king's majesty, his person and authority in the defence and preservation of the foresaid true religion, liberties and laws of the kingdom; as also to the mutual defence and assistance every one of us of another, in the same cause of maintaining the true religion, and his majesty's authority with our best counsel, our bodies, means and whole power, against all sorts of persons whatsoever.

Extract from The National Covenant, 1638, promising to maintain the king's authority and the true (ie Presbyterian) religion.

MONTROSE RETURNED in 1636 to a nation that was deeply divided. In the previous century, the Reformation had swept away the authority of the pre-Reformation Catholic Church in Scotland. Unfortunately, its characteristic greed, self-righteousness and abuse of power was adopted by those that took over the old religious structure.

Two thirds of the lands, rich abbeys and treasure of the pre-Reformation Church fell into the hands of the Scottish nobility who added them to their estates and gained the right to appoint local clergy. Montrose himself inherited estates near Braco that his ancestors had taken from the old bishopric of Dunblane sixty years before.

The new Scottish Presbyterian Kirk had been conceived as a democratic reaction to the hierarchical Catholic Church. In theory, it replaced the authority of the Pope with the authority of the Bible. In practice, it became as powerful a vehicle for oppression and abuse as its predecessor. All depended on who was in control.

John Buchan, in his magisterial biography of *The Marquis of Montrose*, published in 1913, sums up that era of the Scottish Presbyterian Kirk as well as anyone has ever done:

'It sought to make rules for daily life out of the fierce ritual of early Israel. It forgot the spirit in the letter and religion in its mechanical forms. We need not blame the Scottish ministers unduly. Their fashion was the fashion of the age. If man believes that his heart is desperately wicked, that he is doomed to eternal fires but for the interposition of God's grace, and that to walk in grace it is necessary to observe half-understood precepts from the Scriptures without any attempt to rethink them in the light of new conditions – nay, that such an attempt is in God's eyes an unpardonable sin – it is small wonder if he forge such an instrument as the seventeenth century Scottish Kirk. To him, tolerance is only another name for lukewarmness, and reason only the temptation of the devil. If he is right, all those who differ from him must be wrong, and it is his duty to enforce his faith with fire and sword. Since God orders all things, no part of life is beyond the province of His servants, and the Kirk must rule not only in general assemblies but in court and camp and parliament.'

Whoever controlled the Kirk controlled the minds of the Scottish people. Although the Stewart kings had moved their court to London, they had no intention of giving up their control of Scottish religion. James VI argued in his *Trew Law of Free Monarchies* and *Basilikon Doron* that, since the King held his authority by divine right, his word was law in matters of religion as in everything else. The doctrine of the divine right of kings was theoretically compatible with a Kirk whose sole authority was the Bible, since King and Bible were agents of the same God. In practice, the way was open for the usual opportunists to seek power for themselves.

I hear some say, Minister, for all you are saying, the mountain will not come down at this time; ye think nothing, but it will come down. I assure you, I will have it down but ye must not think us that silly, as to think it will come down because we have many for us; we trust not in men but in God; and if this be the time that God will have it down, although ye should lay all your hands about their head, they shall come down; it appears they will come down, if there were no more but their pride, avarice, cruelty and loose living to pull them down, especially when all these are come to height, as they are come to in them. And so much for the mountain; ye see we have reproved it, God remove it.

Extract from a sermon preached by the covenanting minister Andrew Cant 13 June 1638, sure that God was on his side and would move the mountain of Charles I's intransigence.

James VI had died in 1625. His son Charles I inherited the joint crowns of Scotland and England, but had not come to Scotland for a coronation until 1633. By this time, he had made himself thoroughly unpopular by increasing taxation and, worst of all in Scottish eyes, acting like an Englishman. Along with his taste for fashionable frilly manners at court went a preference for the elaborate trappings of the Anglican Episcopal Church rather than the austere regime of the Scottish Presbyterian Kirk.

At the West Port His Majesty had an eloquent speech, making him welcome and the keys of the town offered him by the speaker. As he entered in, and upon the south side of the same Port, Alexander Clerk, then provost of Edinburgh, with the baillies all clad in red robes well furred, and about three score of the aldermen and councillors clad all in black velvet gowns, were sitting all upon seats of deal for the purpose, bigged of three degrees [a three-tier grandstand] from

The high & mighty Monarch. CHARLES by & grace of GOD King of Great Brittaine France & Ireland Defendor of the Faith. etc.

EDYNBURGH

King Charles I visiting Edinburgh in 1633.

Engraving by Cornelius Van Dalen.

which they all rose in great humility and reverence to His Majesty: and the said Alexander Clerk, Provost, in name of the rest, and town of Edinburgh, made some short speech and therewith presented to His Majesty a basin all of gold, estimate to 5000 merks, wherein was shaken out of an embroidered purse a thousand gold double angels, as ane token of the town of Edinburgh their love and humble service. The King looked gladly upon the speech and the gift both, but the Marquis of Hamilton, Master of His Majesty's Horse, had beside meddled with the gift, as due to him by virtue of his office.

Thereafter the Provost went to his horse in good order, having ane rich saddle, with a black velvet footmantle with passments of gold and the rest of the furniture conform, who with the Baillies and Councillors on their foot attended His Majesty. As His Majesty was going to the Upper Bow, there came ane brave company of the town's soldiers, all clad in white satin doublets, black velvet breeches and silk stockings, with hats, feathers, scarves, bands and the rest correspondent [matching]. Their gallants had dainty muskets, pikes and gilded partisans, and such like who guarded His Majesty, having the partisans nearest to him, from place to place, while he came to the Abbey. At the west end of the Tolbooth he saw the royal pedigree of the Kings of Scots, from Fergus the First, delicately painted: and there he had a fourth speech. At the Mercat Cross he had a fifth speech, where His Majesty's health was heartily drunken by Bacchus on the Cross, and the whole stroups [spouts of a fountain] running over with wine in abundance. At the Tron, Parnassus Hill was curiously erected, all green with birks, where nine pretty boys, representing the nine nymphs or Muses, was nymph-like clad.

Charles I's entry into Edinburgh in June 1633 before his coronation, as described by John Spalding, Commissary Clerk of Aberdeen. Montrose was not there to see the pageant. He was travelling in Europe.

Not only did his coronation ritual smack of popery but, the following year, Charles I ordered the Kirk to adopt a new English-style prayer book, full of saints' days and alien symbols such as allowing the minister to turn his back on the congregation during holy communion rather than being one of many democratically assembled round the common table.

By the time Montrose returned from his European travels in 1636, these symbols had become the focus for a more real underlying discontent. The burden of heavy taxation had been worsened by an outflow to England of much of the Scottish nobility, taking their fortunes with them. Judges had been removed from the Privy Council and replaced by bishops. Scotland was governed from afar by a vain, arbitrary, unfeeling monarch and his greedy, sycophant court. Conditions were ripe for revolt.

Montrose had been snubbed by Charles when he was presented at court, but that did not in any way reduce his loyalty to the crown. With his family's long-term view of history, he believed that good and bad kings might come and go but the monarchy itself remained a divine institution. On the other hand, if any king chose to exercise his power badly, it was the duty of his loyal servants to point out the error of his ways.

When Montrose pointed out an error, he did so in no uncertain terms:

Our nation was reduced to almost irreparable evil by the perverse practices of the sometimes pretended prelates [bishops]; who having abused lawful authority, did not only usurp to be lords over God's inheritance, but also intruded themselves in prime places of civil government; ... the very life of the Gospel [was] stolen away by enforcing on the Kirk a dead service book, the brood of the bowels of the Whore of Babel.

On 15 November 1637 Montrose was elected to The Tables, a committee of sixteen that represented Scottish nobility, commoners and Kirk clergy, monitoring the actions of King Charles I and his council.

Every political movement needs its manifesto. Two hard-line Presbyterians, Rev. Alexander Henderson and the lawyer Archibald Johnston of Warriston, drafted the National Covenant, a long-winded document spelling out the grievances caused by the king's policies, swearing allegiance to the king but demanding that Kirk and parliament should not be tampered with.

The Lord has led us hitherto by the hand from step to step; and at every step we would have stood at, made our adversaries to refuse and made us go up a new step of reformation; so even yet in this business, he will not suffer any manner of composition [compromise] or condescendence till he bring us to the highest step of reformation; and, instead of those cautions and limitations of the prelates now contained in our articles, suffer us not to settle till we speak plain truth according to the will of God, that is the utter overthrow and ruin of Episcopacy, that great grandmother of all our corruptions, novations, usurpations, diseases and troubles.

Extract from the Diary of Johnston of Warriston, 4 May 1638, showing that privately his political agenda was already far more extreme than he showed publicly in the legalese of the National Covenant.

Montrose was one of the first to sign on 28 February 1638. Many other Scots nobles followed, including the Marquis of Argyll, an ambitious politician and head of the labyrinthine Campbells. The king saw the National Covenant as treasonous dissent and sent the Marquis of Hamilton to talk to Montrose and other Covenanter leaders.

The talks failed. Hamilton promptly advised the king to place troops in Carlisle and Berwick and send a fleet north, ready to invade Scotland in case of armed rebellion. When war did break out, it was no clear-cut conflict between king and people, but a violent splintering of Scotland into old factions. Argyll mustered Campbell troops in the west. Their traditional enemies,

Reverend Alexander Henderson, co-author of The National Covenant.
Engraved by G. J. Stoddart.

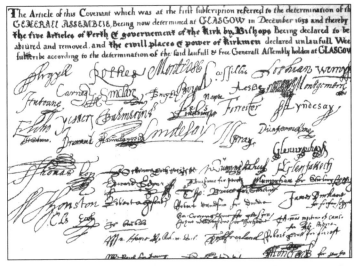

The signatures on The National Covenant with those of Montrose and Argyll on the top line.

the MacDonalds, seized their opportunity to attack Campbell lands. The vacillating Earl of Huntly began to rally the Gordons in the north. Edinburgh seethed with deals and double-deals.

What was Argyll like? The Campbells have always had a reputation for guile and greed. A contemporary poem spells out, in biblical terms, what sort of man Argyll was. It is unlikely that the poem was written by Montrose, though it has many of his mannerisms and argumentative wit.

The poem is a transcription of an oral piece whose puns work out loud. The name Campbell is variously split into 'calm', 'Ham' (son of Noah) and both the Kirk bell and the demon Beelzebub. 'Shem' is both a son of Noah and a term for a confession of faith. The Daniel in the lion's den is Montrose. Gyle puns on guile and Argyll.

The main poem is followed by an ironic answer, which shows that, for all his faults, 'Campbell shall be freer still than Graham'.

PASQUIL ON ARGYLL.

C am is thy name. Cam are thine eyes and ways,
  And with thy Bell thou trawls all traitors to thee.
Cam are thy looks, thine eyes. Thy way bewrays.
Thy strained Bell has witched the vulgar to thee.
Cam's deepest plots excused by declaration.
No sound but Campbell heard throughout our nation.
Cham was a sinner, yet in the Ark preserved.
Bell was a god and needs must be adored,
Whose backdoors Daniel to the king did try
For which he got the den. You may apply.
Then cursed Cham, but thrice most blessed Shem.
He saw and laughed. Thou hid thy father's shame;
And blessed Daniel, altho' thou got the den.
When blinded people see Bell bear the blame,
Campbell begone, for gyle can have no grace.
The righteous suffer for their country's peace.

ANSWER.

T hou gives the prickles and obscures the rose.
  That's treachery to a right-smelling nose.
Yet you're outseen by Cam, your gross mistake;
And the joined Bell may you ere long awake
To your wronged senses, without gyle nor shame;
For Campbell shall be freer still than Graham.

Archibald Campbell, Marquis of Argyll.

Engraved by S. Freeman.

Hamilton sailed north despite a warning from his own mother that she would personally shoot him if he set foot ashore. He persuaded the Gordons to face Montrose who defeated their forces on 18 June 1639 at the Brig o' Dee, the first battle of the Civil War. Montrose entered Aberdeen and managed to prevent his army from sacking the city. Given that his four thousand men were fighting from a variety of motivations, this was a considerable tribute to his powers of command and his distaste for vindictive looting.

Montrose spelled out his perception of the Covenanters' constitutional arguments ina letter of about 1640 to an unknown recipient, possibly the Duke of Lennox:

The perpetual cause of the controversies between the prince and his subjects is the ambitious designs of rule in great men, veiled under the specious pretext of religion and the subjects' liberties, seconded with the arguments and false positions of seditious preachers. First: that the king is ordained for the people and the end is more noble than the means; Second: that the constitutor is superior to the constituted; Third: that the king and his people are two contraries, like the two scales of a balance when the one goes up the other goes down; Fourth: that the prince's prerogative and the people's privilege are incompatible; Fifth: what power is taken from the king is added to the estates of the people. This is the language of the spirits of division that walk betwixt the king and his people, to separate them whom God hath conjoined (which must not pass without some answer) to slide upon which sandy grounds these giants, who war against the Gods, have built their Babel.

In 1639 Montrose saw himself as the loyal subject of an ill-advised king. How did others see him? To Charles I, under the influence of Hamilton, Montrose was a traitor. To the scheming Argyll, he was a dangerous and charismatic rival for the leadership of the covenanters. To the hard-line Presbyterians,

The Signing of the National Covenant in Greyfriars Churchyard,
Edinburgh. 1638.

Engraved by G. Greatbach.

Warriston and Henderson, Montrose was a useful rallying point for troops but too independent of mind. In 1640, Montrose and other moderate peers signed The Cumbernauld Bond, swearing continued allegiance to both king and covenant, but opposed to the 'particular and indirect practicking of a few'.

Whereas we under-subscribers, out of our duty to religion, king and country, were forced to join ourselves in a covenant for the maintenance and defence of eithers, and every one of other in that behalf: Now, finding how that, by the particular and indirect practicking of a few, the country and cause now depending does so much suffer, do heartily bind and oblige ourselves, out of our duty to all these respects above mentioned, but chiefly and mainly that Covenant which we have so solemnly sworn and already signed, to wed and study all public ends which may tend to the safety both of religion, laws and liberties of this poor kingdom.

Extract from the Cumbernauld Bond of August 1640, signed by Montrose and about twenty other Scottish peers, reaffirming their faith in the moderate explicit principles of The National Covenant and opposing themselves to the private extreme political agendas and 'practicking' of Argyll and his followers.

Montrose's army swept south into England. In 1640, he occupied Newcastle and took control of London's vital coal supply. It was a skilful manoeuvre, bringing Scotland's problems home to the London court. Meantime, Argyll led an army through the southern Highlands, settling old Campbell scores and building up his power base. The king weakened. Through the Treaty of Ripon in October 1640, the Scottish parliament won the right to approve royal appointments. The Argyll parliamentary faction was stronger than ever. The Cumbernauld Bond was discovered and burned. Montrose was arrested as an enemy of the state.

IV

CIVIL WAR

M ONTROSE SPENT FIVE months in prison. He was released in November 1641, after Charles I finally agreed to visit Scotland on terms dictated by the Scottish parliament. The King's visit did nothing to defuse the constitutional divisions that threatened the rest of his kingdom. He brought with him Hamilton, who promptly signed the Covenant and wheedled his way into Argyll's favour, while still protesting loyalty to the king.

In England, the shrewd parliamentarian John Pym and the grimly efficient Oliver Cromwell led the opposition to arbitrary royal rule. When civil war broke out in England in 1642, the puritan parliamentary faction was the natural ally of the Scottish Kirk. Warriston and Henderson, the covenanting political theorists, became more extreme. A new manifesto, the Solemn League and Covenant, was drafted in 1643 with the objective of wiping out Catholicism and English episcopacy in Scotland by force, marginalizing the constitutional monarchy. Kirk democracy was being transformed into puritan republicanism.

> **We shall, with the same sincerity, reality and constancy, in our several vocations, endeavour, with our estates and lives, mutually to preserve the rights and privileges of the parliaments, and the liberties of the kingdoms; and to preserve and defend the king's majesty's person and authority in the preservation and defence of the true religion, and liberties of the kingdoms.**
>
> Extract from the Solemn League and Covenant 1643, showing how far the covenanters position had moved from the National Covenant of 1638. The rights of parliaments (of both Scotland and England) are now the priority and the king's authority and personal safety is to be defended only if he in turn defends the true (Presbyterian) religion and the freedom of Kirk and parliaments.

It was no longer possible to be a loyal subject of the king and to obey the narrowing regime of the Kirk. Montrose refused to sign the Solemn League and Covenant, recognising it as a cynical self-justification for the political ambitions of Argyll and the spite of the Kirk. Plot and counterplot swirled. Hamilton aligned himself with Argyll and promised Charles peace in Scotland. Having bought himself time, Argyll merely strengthened his own position till the Scottish parliament was in his pocket and a broad but brittle network of military strength defended his interests. A furious Charles I imprisoned Hamilton and in 1644 raised Montrose from an Earl to a Marquis and made him Lieutenant Governor and Captain General in Scotland. Montrose and his former covenanting allies were now on opposite sides.

While all this was going on, Montrose's wife Magdalen was at home with their children. Her father, the Earl of Southesk, shared Montrose's loyalty to the monarchy but, from the very start of the troubles, disagreed with the Covenanters. Magdalen had seen her friend, Lady Helen Ogilvie, driven heavily pregnant from her home, Airlie Castle, by Argyll while his troops hunted for her husband. There was good reason for Montrose's family to fear the same fate. Montrose's homes in Auld Montrose, Mugdock and Kincardine Castle had already been ransacked in 1641 while he was held in prison in Edinburgh.

Just as Montrose had married the girl next door in Magdalen, so his sister Dorothy had married the boy

Highland targe.
Upper figure shows grasps and screw-in spike sheathed on back of shield.

next door, Sir James Rollo, whose estates adjoined Kincardine. But when she died in 1638, Rollo married Argyll's half-sister Lady Mary Campbell. The next door neighbour was now brother-in-law to Montrose's worst enemy.

Magdalen had borne Montrose two more sons, Robert and David, and a daughter, Jean, after Montrose's return from his European travels. David had died in infancy. There was no way that Montrose could protect Magdalen and their four remaining children while he was away fighting for the king.

Out of the complex troubles of Scotland and the difficulties of his own domestic circumstances, Montrose wrote one of the greatest political poems of all time, all the more poignant in that it is a love poem as well. The poem's second verse contains his most famous lines on courage and integrity.

This is not a smoothly reasoned piece of propaganda from a theoretician, but an impassioned plea by a man of action involved to the point of life or death. He tries to make sense of a personal relationship under pressure from outside events. It is also addressed to the Scotland that he loved and desperately wanted to respect.

His old model of honourable conquest, Alexander the Great, appears in contrast to the Synod, which Montrose despised as a vehicle for the worst kind of collective hypocrisy, and the English republican Commonwealth, a committee-driven abnegation of personal responsibility.

We do not know how close Montrose and Magdalen were by now. There are hints in the poem that he doubted her loyalty, but his message is that his faithfulness can only be deflected by a change of heart on her part. The same is true for Scotland. The first part of the poem is challenging, but optimistic. The second, perhaps written much later, invokes the turtle dove, symbol of faithfulness in grief, and is more sombre.

TO HIS MISTRESS.

To the tune of 'I'll never love thee more'.

PART FIRST.

My dear and only love, I pray
This noble world of thee
Be governed by no other sway
But purest monarchy.
For if confusion have a part,
Which virtuous souls abhor,
And hold a Synod in thy heart,
I'll never love thee more.

Like Alexander I will reign,
And I will reign alone.
My thoughts shall evermore disdain
A rival on my throne.
He either fears his fate too much
Or his deserts are small
That puts it not unto the touch
To win or lose it all.

But I must rule and govern still
And always give the law,
And have each subject at my will
And all to stand in awe.
But 'gainst my battery if I find
Thou shun'st a prize so sore
As that thou sets me up a blind
I'll never love thee more.

Or in the empire of thy heart,
Where I should solely be,
Another do pretend a part
And dares to vie with me,
Or if Committees thou erect
And go on such a score
I'll sing and laugh at thy neglect
And never love thee more.

But if thou wilt be constant then
And faithful of thy word,
I'll make thee glorious by my pen
And famous by my sword.
I'll serve thee in such noble ways
Was never heard before:
I'll crown and deck thee all with bays
And love thee evermore.

PART SECOND.

My dear and only love, take heed
Lest thou thyself expose
And let all longing lovers feed
Upon such looks as those.
A marble wall then build about;
myself shall be the door.
But if thou let thy heart fly out,
I'll never love thee more.

Let not their oaths, like volleys shot,
Make any breach at all;
Nor smoothness of their language plot
Which way to scale the wall;
Nor balls of wild-fire love consume
The shrine which I adore.
For if such smoke about thee fume,
I'll never love thee more.

I think thy virtues be too strong
To suffer by surprise;
Which, victual'd by my love so long,
Their siege at length must rise,
And leave thee ruled in that health
And state thou wast before.
But if thou turn a Common-wealth
I'll never love thee more.

But if, by fraud or by consent,
Thy heart to ruin come,
I'll sound no trumpet as I wont,
Nor march by tuck of drum;
But hold my arms, like ensigns, up
Thy falsehood to deplore,
And bitterly will sigh and weep
And never love thee more.

I'll do with thee as Nero did
When Rome was set on fire;
Not only all relief forbid,
But to a hill retire;
And scorn to shed a tear to see
Thy spirit grown so poor;
But, smiling, sing until I die,
'I'll never love thee more'.

Yet for the love I bare thee once,
Lest that thy name should die,
A monument of marble stone
The truth shall testify;
That every pilgrim passing by
May pity and deplore
My case, and read the reason why
I'll never love thee more.

The golden laws of love shall be
Upon this pillar hung;
A simple heart, a single eye,
A true and constant tongue.
Let no man for more love pretend
Than he has hearts in store;
True love begun shall never end.
Love one and love no more.

Then shall thy heart be set by mine,
But in far different case;
For mine was true, so was not thine,
But look'd like Janus' face.
For as the waves on every wind
So sails thou every shore
And leaves my constant heart behind.
How can I love thee more?

My heart shall with the sun be fix'd
For constancy most strange;
And thine shall with the moon be mix'd
Delighting aye in change.
Thy beauty shin'd at first most bright,
And woe is me therefore
That ever I found thy love so light,
I could love thee no more.

The misty mountains, smoking lakes,
The rocks' resounding echo,
The whistling wind that murmur makes,
Shall with me sing Hey ho.
The tossing seas, the tumbling boats,
Tears dropping from each shore,
Shall tune with me their turtle notes;
'I'll never love thee more'.

As doth the turtle chaste and true
Her fellow's death regret,
And daily mourns for his adieu
And ne'er renews her mate;
So, though thy faith was never fast,
Which grieves me wondrous sore,
Yet shall I live in love so chaste,
That I shall love no more.

And when all gallants ride about
These monuments to view,
Whereon is written in and out
Thou traitorous and untrue;
Then in a passion they shall pause
And thus say, sighing sore,
Alas! He had too just a cause
Never to love thee more.

And when the tracing goddess, Fame,
From east to West shall flee,
She shall record it to thy shame,
How thou hast loved me;
And how in odds our love was such,
As few have been before;
Thou loved too many and I too much,
That I can love no more.

Charles I had made Montrose Lieutenant Governor and Captain General of his army in Scotland, but lacked the resources to equip him for the task in hand. By the summer of 1644, Argyll had crushed a royalist rising in the north. All royalist troops from the south of Scotland

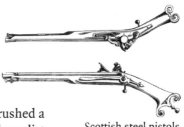

Scottish steel pistols.

were diverted to help the king's cause in England. Where was the new Captain General to find an army?

The Earl of Antrim had promised the king an army of ten thousand Irish MacDonalds. Only two thousand turned up, led by the formidable Alastair MacDonald, who had not been told about Montrose's new command status. In the eyes of the Covenanter – dominated Scottish Parliament, Montrose was an outlaw. Montrose secretly made his way home to Perthshire, accompanied by only two companions. He met Alastair in Blair Atholl and raised the royal standard. Within days, he added to the hungry MacDonald army a band of eight hundred Atholl Highlanders plus a host of Grants, Robertsons and Mackenzies who had just seen their farms pillaged by Argyll. It was a small, miscellaneous army, but with it Montrose won an astonishing series of victories that established his reputation as a great military strategist and brilliant tactician.

On 1 September 1644 he advanced on Perth. Within sight of his late mother's castle of Huntingtower, he crushed the Covenanters at the Battle of Tippermuir. Their leader, Lord Elcho, fled leaving two thousand of his men dead and another thousand prisoner.

As soon as they were within cannon-shot, the enemy, under Lord Drummond, sent out some picked men to skirmish with Montrose and harass his line. To check them he despatched a small body who, at the first onset, threw them into disorder, routed them and drove them back in panic to their own line.

Montrose seized the decisive moment to charge. Nothing could animate his men and strike terror into the enemy more effectually than an immediate attack while they were still confused and dismayed at their first blow, before they had time to rally or recover courage. With a loud cheer he hurled his whole line upon them. The enemy discharged their canon which were planted in front, but at such a distance that they produced more noise than execution. Then they advanced and their horse moved forward to attack. But Montrose's men, though their powder was spent, and few of them were armed with pikes or even swords, received them boldly with such weapons as fell to hand, namely stones no less of which they poured in heavy volleys with such force and spirit that they compelled them to sound a retreat and trouble them no more.

The Irish and Highlanders in gallant rivalry behaved with the utmost courage and pressed so hard on their retreat that at last they broke and fled. On the right wing the engagement lasted longer. Here James Scott for some time made a desperate effort to gain the higher ground. But Montrose's men, who were superior in strength of body, and especially in speed and agility, seized the position. Then the Atholl men charged down with drawn claymores and, unchecked by a hail of bullets from the musketeers, they closed with them slashing and cutting down all before them.

Unable to stand the shock, the enemy at last fairly fled away.

> Most of the cavalry saved themselves by the speed of their horses, but among the foot there was a very great slaughter, as the conquerors pursued them for six or seven miles. Two thousand covenanters are said to have been slain and a larger number captured. Some of them took the oath of service and enlisted with the victor; but nearly all of them broke their word and deserted.
>
> *George Wishart (chaplain to Montrose) describing the Battle of Tippermuir. 1644.*

On 13 September, he won the Battle of Aberdeen. Five years previously, he had managed to stop his troops from sacking the city. This time, the Irish MacDonalds ran amok. Montrose was appalled by the looting, raping and killing but, for one hideous night, his army was out of control. He never let it happen again.

For the next six weeks, Montrose's army marched through Aberdeenshire, Perthshire and Angus, trying to restore royal authority. On 28 October, Montrose faced Argyll himself at the Battle of Fyvie, north of Aberdeen. The Covenanters were repelled. Argyll asked for a truce and promptly tried to persuade the Irish troops to hand over Montrose who had a price of £20,000 on his head, dead or alive. They remained loyal. Montrose's little army headed south back to Atholl.

What happened next was extraordinary. As winter closed in, Montrose led his men through the mountainous west of Scotland into the heart of Campbell country and took them by surprise. Alastair's MacDonalds wreaked havoc on the homesteads of their traditional clan enemy. Argyll fled by sea, only to send a huge covenanting army to face Montrose at Inverlochy on 3 February 1645. Montrose's men slaughtered them.

Iron hat of Charles I.

Montrose's eldest son, John, aged fourteen, joined him for the campaign in the west, but after Inverlochy he fell ill and died. The next month, his twelve year old brother James, now heir to the Montrose title, was seized by the Covenanters from his mother's home in Auld Montrose and imprisoned in Edinburgh Castle. Magdalen's fears for her family were now a reality.

Montrose could do nothing but press on with his campaign. On 4 April 1645, he won a narrow victory at Dundee, then a thorough one at Auldearn, near Inverness on 9 May. On 10 July, the covenanters were routed at Alford, near Aberdeen, and again on 15 August at Kilsyth, from where Montrose rode into Glasgow at the head of his victorious men. He managed to prevent his Irish troops from sacking the city.

First, by his long imprisonment his body is visibly decayed and pined away, and the strength thereof altogether abated, so that he is not able himself to stand or walk. Next, there is only one boy to attend him, whose father lately died of the pest [plague], with whom the said boy was shortly before his decease. Thirdly, the house where he was furnished his meat and drink is infected and diverse persons therein died of the plague, and by the visitation of the town of Edinburgh, there is few left of that sort who can or will afford him any entertainment, and many times he will be forty-eight hours without so much as one cup of cold water: and which distress is likely to increase.

Petition from Lady Ogilvie to the Scottish Parliament in August 1645 to have her husband removed from the plague-ridden Edinburgh Tolbooth to another prison. Parliament, knowing that Montrose's troops were advancing south, tactfully consented to Lord Ogilvie's being moved to the cleaner Bass Rock prison. Before he could be transferred, Montrose won the Battle of Kilsyth and achieved the release of most royal prisoners, including Ogilvie.

Within a year Montrose had risen from being a hunted outlaw with only two companions to having real political and military authority. The title given him by the king, Lieutenant Governor and Captain General in Scotland, now had some substance.

Victory was far from complete. Montrose went to Edinburgh and succeeded in releasing most royalist prisoners, except for those, including his young heir James, who were held in the grimly defended Edinburgh Castle.

Montrose's Irish troops, disgruntled by their lack of plunder from Glasgow and lacking the motivation of more Campbell blood to shed, melted away home. Montrose's Gordon troops, whose allegiance was never certain under the wavering Earl of Huntly, also headed home.

Montrose was now faced with two bad options. He could retreat back to the Highlands with his remaining men, abandoning the Lowlands to the regrouping Covenanters, or he could press on and try to take southern Scotland for the king. Typically, he chose 'to win or lose it all'.

He led his depleted army into the Borders where they were intercepted on 13 September 1645 at Philiphaugh, near Selkirk, by the most able of the covenanting generals, David Leslie, at the head of a large, well-equipped army. This time, courage and tactical skill were not enough. Leslie's disciplined cavalry and professional footsoldiers outnumbered and overran Montrose's remaining Irish troops and Highlanders, inflicting severe losses. Montrose fought on as long as he could, then reluctantly ordered retreat.

The Covenanters took horrific revenge on royalist women and other non-combatants. Pregnant Irish women were particularly singled out and hacked open till their foetuses fell to the ground. Cooks and children were raped and slaughtered. Some who fled north were rounded up and taken to the bridge at Linlithgow where they were thrown into the River Avon. Those who survived were stabbed back into the water by rows of covenanting pikemen until all drowned.

The triumphant Kirk demanded that all royalist captives should be killed. Montrose's surviving Irish soldiers were lined up, shot and thrown into mass graves. Argyll's Kirk cronies rounded up royalist nobles and executed them with a cold, systematic malevolence that left a permanent stain on the reputation of the Church in Scotland.

Sir Robert Spottiswoode, who was a royalist sympathiser but had no record of taking arms against the Covenanters, was executed like many of his kind. The night before he died, he wrote to Montrose, entrusting his children to Montrose's care, and asking him 'as you have always done hitherto, so you will continue by fair and gentle carriage to gain the people's affection to their Prince, rather than to imitate the barbarous inhumanity of your adversaries, although they give your Excellence too great provocations to follow their example'. Montrose's code of honour held good. There were no reprisals.

In March 1646, Montrose's own Kincardine Castle, near Auchterarder, was reduced to rubble by heavy cannon brought from Stirling. In November, his wife Magdalen died. Montrose had her buried at their surviving home in Auld Montrose. Her father, Lord Southesk, took care of young Robert and Jean. Montrose's heir James, now aged 14, was still a prisoner in Edinburgh Castle.

In the spring of 1646, Montrose was trying to raise a new royalist army in the Highlands when he received a letter from King Charles I saying, 'You must disband your forces and go to France where you shall receive my further directions.'

Charles was losing the Civil War in England and had been negotiating with the French to intervene on his behalf. He had fallen into the hands of the covenanting army at Newark and was sold to the English parliamentarian army like a prize pig.

Charles's only hope for Scotland was to get Montrose out safely to try again another day. Montrose refused to abandon his army, knowing what the Kirk was capable of doing to defence-

The Battle of Philiphaugh.

It usually happens that those who leave the right road and wander off the king's highways get lost in a labyrinth of devious and entangled by-paths. This we find by sad experience has been the case of the fanatical reformers. Under pretext of restoring religion, they have not only shaken but shattered both church and state...

Into their meeting, which they call their presbytery, they co-opt such of the people as are most zealous for their way, chapmen, ploughmen, mechanics, sailors, tailors, colliers, cobblers, and the like, without [holy] orders, and without instruction in sacred mysteries. These have the same right to vote as the ministers themselves. They are elected annually, and dignified with the title of lay or ruling elders. Among their ministers they pretend to maintain complete equality, a mere fiction, upset in practice. Their real rulers are a small clique, advanced by the popular applause and the giddy conceit of the rabble, who lord it most tyrannically, not only over their brethren, but over peers of the realm and even the king himself.

George Wishart. Deeds of Montrose, 1649, giving a royalist view of covenanting involvement in church and state.

less enemies. He negotiated a surrender at Rattray in Perthshire with a pardon for all but himself and a few others. On 3 September 1646, Montrose and his remaining followers set sail for Europe.

V

EXILE

He was an accomplished gentleman of many excellent parts: a body not tall, but comely and well composed in all his lineaments: his complexion merely white, with flaxen hair: of a staid, grave and solid look, and yet his eyes sparkling and full of life: of speech slow, but witty and full of sense; a presence graceful, courtly and so winning upon the beholder as it seemed to claim reverence without asking for it: for he was so affable, so courteous and so benign, as seemed verily to scorn ostentation and the keeping of state [class rank], and therefore he quickly made a conquest of the hearts of all his followers, so as when he list [liked] he could have led them in a chain to have followed him with cheerfulness in all his enterprises: and I am certainly persuaded that his gracious, humane and courteous freedom of behaviour, being certainly acceptable before God and man, was it that won him so much renown, and enabled him chiefly, in the love of his followers, to go through so great enterprise.

Extract from Sir Patrick Gordon of Ruthven's 'A Short Abridgement of Britane's Distemper from the Year of God 1630 to 1649', showing how Montrose's charisma stemmed from his clear distinction between any individual's social status and his true worth. It made his followers feel personally valued and alienated those who regarded themselves as exempt from showing courtesy and compassion because of their self-appointed religious and political agendas.

MONTROSE LANDED IN BERGEN in Norway on 10 September 1646. He wanted to meet with King Christian IV of Denmark, Charles I's uncle, to see if he would lend military aid and set off to meet Christian in Hamburg. Before he could see the Danish king, Montrose received a letter from Charles, telling him to hurry to Paris where he would receive further orders.

In Paris, a British royal court in exile was taking shape with Charles's queen Henrietta Maria at its head. Anne of Austria, mother of the infant king Louis XIV, lent the Louvre to house the courtiers who had fled from London. Pretty manners and petty intrigue unfortunately survived the Channel crossing all too well. The Hamilton faction was well-represented. Lord Jermyn had wormed his way into the Queen's confidence and had control of the much-shrunken royal purse. While he and his cronies chattered and danced, no funds could be found to assist Montrose in raising an army to invade Scotland.

Montrose was never comfortable at court. He was elegant and courteous, rather than foppish and supercilious. He was widely read and direct in his speech at a time when surface and spin were fashionable. Above all, he had a reputation for fiercely defending his unswerving principles. He stood out like a sore thumb among the fickle butterflies that flitted around the remains of the royal honeypot.

Montrose feared for the fate of the royal cause. He looked at the courtiers who purported to be loyal to the king and wrote:

ON THE FAITHLESSNESS AND VENALITY OF HIS TIMES.

Unhappy is the man
In whose breast is confined
The sorrows and distresses all
Of an afflicted mind.

Th' extremity is great;
He dies if he conceal.
The world's so void of secret friends
Betrayed if he reveal.

Then break afflicted heart!
And live not in these days
When all prove merchants of their faith,
None trusts what other says.

For when the sun doth shine,
Then shadows do appear.
But when the sun doth hide his face,
They with the sun retire.

Some friends as shadows are,
And fortune as the sun;
They never proffer any help
Till fortune first begun.

But if in any case
Fortune shall first decay,
Then they, as shadows of the sun,
With fortune run away.

Charles I had promised Montrose the role of Ambassador Extraordinary with the authority to deal with European governments. When he approached the French, he received no offer of aid for Charles I but was instead offered the post of Marshal of France for himself. Many Scottish soldiers had served foreign governments with distinction though never with such a high rank. Montrose was suspicious. The French had been negotiating with the English parliamentary faction and an appointment in the French army would keep Montrose handily out of Britain. He declined the offer.

Instead he sought help from the Holy Roman Empire with whom France was fighting the Thirty Years' War. He went to Vienna then Prague where the Emperor Frederick III made him a Marshal of the Holy Roman Empire with the authority to raise forces in Flanders. The Emperor wrote to his brother, Archduke Leopold, Governor of the Netherlands, instructing him to support Montrose.

Montrose made his way back across a Europe that was plagued by invading armies and marauding gangs. He arrived in Brussels to find that Archduke Leopold had just been heavily defeated by French troops at Lens on 20 August 1648 and was in no position to offer him any aid. The royalist cause in England was in an even worse position. Hamilton's feeble efforts on the king's behalf resulted in defeat by the parliamentary army at Preston and an increasingly powerful Oliver Cromwell went north to discuss with Argyll how their common cause could be best served.

During the winter, it became clear that there was only one remaining obstacle to the Kirk in Scotland and the parliament in England gaining complete authority – the king himself. On 30 January 1649, Charles I was publicly executed in London.

Ironically, Montrose heard the news as he was about to meet the future Charles II who had set up his own court-in-exile at The Hague, away from the bickering shambles of his mother's court-in-exile in Paris.

The king's death chilled Montrose into a terrible fury. Death in battle would have been one thing; cold-blooded judicial murder was the deepest insult to the cavalier code of honour by which his entire life had been conducted. He felt that in the past months he had been like the mythological figure Argus, watching but never acting. Now was the time to be a Briareus, the hundred-handed destroyer. He sat down and wrote:

Oliver Cromwell.

Engraved by E. Scriven.

HIS METRICAL VOW.

G reat! Good! And Just! Could I but rate
My griefs and thy too rigid fate,
I'd weep the world to such a strain
As it should deluge once again.
But, since thy loud-tongued blood demands supplies
More from Briareus hands than Argus eyes,
I'll sing thy obsequies with trumpet sounds
And write thy epitaph in blood and wounds.

This was no idle boast. Montrose's military record was second to none. 'Blood and wounds' were what the king's murderers deserved. He resolved to return to Britain.

Methinks I see in my mind a noble and puissant Nation rousing herself like a strong man after sleep, and shaking her invincible locks. Methinks I see her as an eagle mewing her mighty youth, and kindling her undazzled eyes at the full midday beam, purging and unscaling her long abused sight at the fountain itself of heavenly radiance, while the whole noise of timorous and flocking birds, with those also that love the twilight, flutter about, amazed at what she means, and in their envious gabble would prognosticate a year of sects and schisms.

John Milton, the poet and pamphleteer, welcoming the puritan revolution in his 'Areopagitica' published in 1644. Milton became Latin Secretary to Cromwell's Council of State. 'Areopagitica' contains a plea for the freedom of the press at a time when the crown suppressed what it regarded as seditious tracts. To no-one's surprise, the Puritans attempted the same anti-opposition censorship when they came to power. When Montrose was executed in 1650, his enemies hung round his neck a printed account of his successful campaigns and his poem 'Great! Good! And Just!', published in Amsterdam the previous year and smuggled into Britain.

In England, other executions followed. Hamilton was executed on 9 March 1649. His end was the noblest part of his life, for he refused to betray to Cromwell's men the names of suspected English royalists. Argyll gloated. Another rival was dead.

At The Hague, Montrose made a good friend in Elizabeth, elder sister of Charles I, who had married Frederick, Elector Palatine of the Rhine. Better known as 'The Winter Queen' after Frederick died, she had a good ear for court intrigue and gave Montrose both encouragement and timely warnings. Her son, Prince Rupert of the Rhine, was an outstanding cavalier general. Her younger daughter, Sophie, married the Elector of Hanover. In 1714, Sophie's son succeeded to the thrones of England and Scotland as George I.

One of the intriguing 'what ifs' of history concerns Princess Louise, the Winter Queen's older daughter. She was a shy girl, devoted to painting, who despised superficial courtly manners. She was a pupil of Gerard van Honthorst and it was probably through her advice that Montrose commissioned the Dutch artist to paint the famous portrait of himself, which he gave to Louise's mother. Her younger sister, Sophie's, memoirs hint that Montrose and Louise were in love. If they had married, their heir and not Sophie's would have inherited the English and Scottish thrones.

It was not to be. Montrose decided that his duty lay in raising an army for the new King Charles II. Louise became a nun and lived till 1709.

> These memoirs of Montrose will show your highness [Charles II] what is our greatest hope for your future fortunes – that the Scots have never all been rebels to their most excellent king. To say otherwise is grievously to misrepresent our nation, a cruel and malicious slander of our enemies as unjust to men of honour, ready to suffer hardship in his majesty's cause, as they have been treacherous

and disloyal to your sire and yourself. Their sole aim is to discredit and cripple your friends, servants and most faithful subjects, whose loyalty and courage fills them with evil terror, lest these wicked conspirators should, through them, be forced to pay the due penalties of treason.

Let no caviller declare that we think or speak ill of the most noble nation of England, a charge we abhor with our whole soul. Many of them have aided the king with loyalty and courage to their own eternal glory. This we gladly recognise and declare and congratulate them for it. Only let them treat us with the same justice and candour, and not impute to our whole race the crime of a mere faction, however powerful and great.

Extract from George Wishart's dedication to the future Charles II of his Deeds of Montrose, 1649, reminding the anglicised monarch that not all Scots are alike.

The Covenanters realised too late that a disciplined Lord Protector Cromwell at the head of an English republic was a far greater menace to Scottish independence than a weak remote monarchy. Argyll sent commissioners to The Hague telling the newly bereaved Charles II that he could succeed his father as king in Scotland if he signed the Solemn League and Covenant and dismissed Montrose. When Montrose pointed out to Charles II that signing would entitle him to just the same degree of loyalty that the Covenanters had shown his father, the new king sent the Covenanting delegation away and appointed Montrose Viceroy of Scotland and Captain General of his armies there. It was up to Montrose to raise these armies. He had done so once spectacularly in 1644-45. Could he do it again?

Montrose recruited troops in Holland, Denmark and Sweden. Charles encouraged him to invade Scotland. It was suggested that as many as twenty thousand soldiers could be rallied

King Charles II.
From the painting by Peter Lely.

among the clans in the north. At the same time, Charles was carrying on negotiations with the Covenanters to see whether he could make a better deal. Montrose suspected Charles of duplicity, but obeyed the royal command as he had always done.

My Lord,

I entreat you to go on vigorously and with your wonted courage and care in the prosecution of those trusts I have committed to you, and not to be startled with any reports you may hear, as if I were otherwise inclined to the Presbyterians than when I left you. I assure you I am upon the same principles as I was, and depend as much as ever upon your undertakings and endeavours for my service, being fully resolved to assist and support you therein to the uttermost of my power, as you shall find in effect, when you desire anything to be done by your affectionate friend,

Charles R

St Germains. Sept 19th 1649.

Letter from Charles II to Montrose, telling him not to believe rumours that the king was negotiating with the Covenanters – which is exactly what he was doing.

Montrose was under no illusions about the Stewart monarchy. Both Charles I and Charles II were vain, devious, arbitrary and self-indulgent. In Montrose's mind, however, monarchy was the only true form of government. The horrors brought about by the rule of the Kirk and the parliament had confirmed him in his view. The king's execution on 30 January 1649 had raised questions about the natural order of life and about the love for Scotland that Montrose felt deeply. He wrote:

ON THE DEATH OF CHARLES I.

Burst out my soul in main of tears,
And thou my heart sighs' tempest move;
My tongue let never plaints forbear,
But murmur still my crossed love;
Combine together all in one
And thunder forth my tragic moan.

But tush, poor drop, cut breath, broke air,
Can you my passions express?
No; rather but augment my care
In making them appear the less.
Seeing but from small woes words do come;
And great ones, they sing always dumb.

My swelling grief then bend yourself
This fatal breast of mine to fill,
The centre where all sorrows dwell,
The limbeck where all griefs distill;
That silent thus in plaints I may
Consume and melt myself away.

Yet that I may contented die,
I only wish before my death,
Transparent that my breast may be,
E're that I do expire my breath;
Since sighs, tears, plaints, express no smart,
It might be seen into my heart.

It was time to turn words into deeds. In March 1650 Montrose sailed to Orkney where he assembled a force of around fifteen hundred men. On 12 April, he raised the royal standard at John O'Groats on the mainland of Scotland. The last campaign had begun.

VI

THE FINAL CAMPAIGN

As the nature of foul weather lieth not in a shower or two of rain, but in an inclination thereto of many days together, so the nature of war consisteth not in actual fighting, but in the known disposition thereto during all the time there is no assurance to the contrary. All other time is Peace.

Whatsoever therefore is consequent to a time of War, where every man is enemy to every man, the same is consequent to the time when men live without other security than what their own strength and their own invention shall furnish them withal. In such condition, there is no place for Industry, because the fruit thereof is uncertain: and consequently no culture of the Earth: no Navigation nor use of the commodities that may be imported by Sea: no commodious Building: no instruments of moving, and removing such things as require much force: no Knowledge of the face of the Earth: no account of Time: no Arts: no Letters: no Society: and, which is worst of all, continual fear and danger of violent death: and the life of man, solitary, poor, nasty, brutish and short.

Thomas Hobbes in 'The Leviathan', published in 1651, famously summing up the effects of war. Hobbes served as Charles II's mathematics tutor at the court in exile in Paris.

MONTROSE'S LOYALTY to Charles II was not mutual. Charles I's inflexible assertion of the divine right of kings had led to his execution. His son had no intentions of going the same way as his father. Charles II, from his court in exile in Breda in The Netherlands, was prepared to negotiate with anyone who held real political power and to sacrifice any loyal follower as long as the Stewart dynasty was restored to the pleasures of the court in London.

Montrose before his final campaign.

Engraved by S. Freeman from the painting by Van Dyck.

The Scottish nobles knew that, while Charles was encouraging Montrose to conquer Scotland on his behalf, he was also sounding out Argyll and the Covenanters as to whether they would break off their alliance with Cromwell and the English parliamentarians in exchange for assured political power for the Kirk in Scotland.

Montrose was all too aware that his own military and political resources did not match the commission the king had given him. He wrote:

ON HIS OWN CONDITION.

I would be high, but that the cedar tree
Is blustr'd down while smaller shrubs go free.

I would be low, but that the lowly grass

Is trampled down by each unworthy ass.

For to be high, my means they will not do;

And to be low, my mind it will not bow.

O Heavens! O Fate! When will you once agree

To reconcile my means, my mind and me?

Montrose advanced south from John O'Groats with an army of only sixteen hundred men. Which of the nobles and clansmen would join him? Montrose's code of 'Win or lose it all' had less appeal when the situation was so fluid that no-one could guess the odds on success. Montrose received many promises but few men. Crucially, the Earl of Sutherland decided to back Argyll. Montrose had to divide his meagre forces. He sent his half-brother Harry Graham with troops to keep Sutherland's increasing army occupied. Montrose himself headed south, now with only twelve hundred men, nearly all on foot.

On 27 April 1650, he had only gone as far as Carbisdale when he was surprised by a charge of three hundred cavalry led by Colonel Archibald Strachan. These were crack troops sent ahead by the brilliant Covenanting general David Leslie who had defeated Montrose at Philiphaugh in 1645.

Strachan's cavalry charge broke through with deadly efficiency. Montrose was unable to regroup his men. Within two hours, nine hundred royalists were killed or taken prisoner. The rest were scattered.

Montrose had his horse shot from under him. Wounded, he eluded search parties for two days until he met an apparently friendly ghillie who took him on 29 April to Ardvreck Castle, home of Neil MacLeod of Assynt. He was fed and sheltered. On 4 May, MacLeod handed Montrose over to the Covenanters.

MacLeod received the reward of £20,000, offered for Montrose since 1644, plus a bonus of £5,000 worth of meal. It was a time of famine in the north. MacLeod of Assynt was one of those who adopted a 'wait and see' policy before deciding whether to back the royalists or the Covenanters. He was already under pressure from the Earl of Sutherland. His choice lay between risking his estates by protecting Montrose, who might be unable to raise another army, or to hand him over for money. He took the money, earning himself a place in Scottish legend as the archetypical betrayer.

The captive Montrose was paraded through villages by Major General Holbourn and his Covenanting troops. They expected crowds to jeer at their prisoner. Instead, people stood silent as he rode past, head held high, in chains on a tiny pony.

He was held in respect even in the houses where he was held prisoner on his way south. At Skibo Castle, the formidable Lady Gray swatted Holbourn with a leg of mutton when he insulted Montrose. After this, David Leslie took personal charge of the captive, treating him as an honourable prisoner of war, but could not prevent his being forced to listen to taunting covenanting sermons as he was led through Inverness and Aberdeenshire.

General David Leslie.

Engraved by G. J. Stoddart from the painting by Peter Lely.

Skibo Castle was then occupied by a dowager lady named Gray. On the arrival of the Marquis and his guards, she prepared a suitable entertainment for them. She presided at the dinner table, at the head of which, and immediately before her, was a leg of roasted mutton. When Montrose entered the room he was introduced to her by the officers who escorted him, and she requested him to be seated next to her; but Holbourn, still retaining the strict military order he maintained in his march, placed the Marquis between himself and another officer, and thus he sat down at Lady Skibo's right hand, and above his noble prisoner before the lady was aware of the alteration.

She no sooner observed this arrangement than she flew into a violent passion, seized the leg of roasted mutton by the shank, and hit Holbourn such a notable blow in the head with the flank part of the hot juicy mutton as knocked him off his seat, and completely spoiled his uniform. The officers took alarm, dreading an attempt to rescue the prisoner; but the lady, still in great wrath and brandishing the leg of mutton, reminded them that she received them as guests; that, as such and as gentlemen, they must accommodate themselves to such an adjustment of place at her table as she considered to be correct; that although the Marquis was a prisoner, she was the more resolved to support his rank when unfortunate than if he had been victorious; and consequently that no person of inferior rank could, at her table, be permitted to take precedence of him. Order being restored, and the mutton replaced on the table, every possible civility was thereafter directed by all present to the Marquis.

Extract from Taylor, Dunrobin MS, showing that ladies can be just as gallant as gentlemen and that it is unwise to interfere with Highland manners. Skibo Castle today retains its reputation for newsworthy hospitality.

He was allowed to stop at Kinnaird Castle where his father-in-law, the Earl of Southesk, was caring for his two youngest children, Robert and Jean. He said goodbye to them for the last time. Robert was later to become a soldier and die fighting in Europe. Jean never married. Montrose could not see his other surviving son James, heir to the Montrose title, who was in exile with other Scots in Flanders.

What should Montrose do now? Should he try to save his life by throwing himself on the mercy of parliament and abandon the principles of religious freedom and constitutional monarchy for which he had always fought? It was not in his temperament to be dragged down to the level of his enemies. He wrote:

ON NATURAL ORDER.

C an little beasts with lions roar,
And little birds with eagles soar?
Can shallow streams command the seas,
And little ants the humming bees?
No, no, no, it is not meet
The head should stoop unto the feet.

At Dundee he was put on board a ship for Edinburgh. On 18 May, he was bound in cords and led up the Royal Mile in a cart with a hangman riding on the cart horse. A parliamentary committee tried to hire women to stone him as he passed. Instead they wept at the sight of the quiet, courageous figure on his way to the Tolbooth.

Meantime, Charles II, from the comfort of his court in Breda, was negotiating with the Scottish parliament which was now completely in the control of Argyll and the Covenanters. On 3 May, he sent a letter to Montrose, gratuitously ordering him to abandon his mission in Scotland. By the time Montrose was a prisoner in Edinburgh, Charles had written to the Scottish parliament saying he was ' heartily sorry' that Montrose had invaded Scotland.

Parliament needed no encouragement to dispose of Montrose. He was given no trial. Instead, a death sentence was read to him on 20 May by Johnston of Warriston. Montrose pointed out that everything he had done had been expressly ordered by the king, but he was sent back to his Tolbooth cell to await execution. He was told that he would be hanged like a common criminal, rather than executed on the block like King Charles I, and that his body would be cut up and exhibited throughout Scotland.

That night, Covenanting preachers were sent to torment him. He listened quietly. Jailers were told to make noises to keep him awake and to blow tobacco smoke in his face, because it was known he disliked tobacco ever since he had seen it ruin his father's health.

Eventually, the preachers went home and the jailers dozed off. Montrose wrote a final poem, placing his trust in God rather than in kings:

HIS METRICAL PRAYER BEFORE EXECUTION.

Let them bestow on every airth a limb,
Then open all my veins that I may swim
To thee my Maker in that crimson lake;
Then place my par-boiled head upon a stake;
Scatter my ashes, strew them in the air.
Lord, since thou know'st where all these atoms are,
I'm hopeful thou'lt recover once my dust
And confident thou'lt raise me with the just.

Montrose decided to meet his death, not as a cowed victim, but in a manner fitting to his royal title of Viceroy of Scotland. He dressed as a cavalier in scarlet overlaid with silver lace, with a white linen shirt, white gloves and red silk stockings. He walked to the scaffold on the morning of Tuesday 21 May, hat in hand.

The ministers of the Kirk refused to give him the customary prayer, so Montrose prayed for himself. Argyll watched as his Covenanters reached out to hang round Montrose's neck a book written by George Wishart, Montrose's chaplain, and published in Amsterdam the year before. This *History of the King's Majestie's Affaires* in Scotland recounted Montrose's victories and his loyalty to the monarchy. It is prefaced by his poem *Great! Good! And Just!*.

The Covenanters had intended the display of Montrose's poem round his hanged neck as a justification for their sneering triumphalism. The crowd saw it as a badge of honour.

His last words, as he stood on the gallows with his hands tied behind his back, were, 'May God have mercy on this afflicted Kingdom.'

After hanging for three hours, his body was cut down and quartered. His head was stuck on a spike on the Edinburgh Tolbooth, his arms and legs were sent for display in Scottish cities and his trunk was dumped in a short box on the Boroughmuir.

LAMENT FOR MONTROSE.

I'll not go to Dunedin
Since the Graham's blood was shed,

The manly mighty lion

Tortured on the gallows.

That was the true gentleman
Who came of line not humble,
Good was the flushing of his cheek
When dawn up to combat.

His chalk-white teeth well-closing,
His slender brow not gloomy;
Though oft my love awakes me,
This night I will not bear it.

Neil's son of woeful Assynt,
If I in net could take thee,
My sentence would condemn thee,
Nor would I spare the gibbet.

If you and I encountered
On the marshes of Ben Etive,
The black water and the clods
Would there be mixed together.

If thou and thy wife's father,
The householder of Lemlair,
Were hanged both together,
'Twould not atone my loss.

Stript tree of the false apples,
Without esteem or fame or grace,
Ever murdering each other,
Mid dregs of wounds and knives.

> Death-wrapping to thee, base one!
>
> Ill didst thou sell the righteous,
>
> For the meal of Leith,
>
> And two-thirds of it sour!
>
> By the great Gaelic poet, Ian Lom, published in 1652 and translated by Alexander Nicholson.

On 1 January 1651 at Scone, Argyll placed the crown of Scotland on the head of Charles II. Now that he had been formally crowned, Charles promptly withdrew back to the safety of Europe while Scotland fell apart in a welter of blood-letting that lasted until 1660.

Argyll's power was finally broken by his former allies of the English parliamentary party which had become the Commonwealth, with Oliver Cromwell as its Lord Protector. Cromwell sent General Monk in 1654 to ravage Argyll territory much as Montrose had done at Inverlochy.

When Oliver Cromwell died in 1658, his son Richard succeeded him as Lord Protector. It was the best thing that could have happened for the monarchy. Richard had no taste for violence or political intrigue and retired to France in 1660.

Charles II's appetite for intrigue never left him. In 1660 he returned to Britain as ruling monarch and dealt with his enemies. Johnston of Warriston, the fanatic architect of the Covenants who had delighted in reading Montrose's death sentence to him, was himself executed, though he tried to avoid sentence by pretending to be insane.

All that remained was for Charles II to shed crocodile tears and stage a magnificent funeral for Montrose eleven years after his death.

Most of Montrose's remains were recovered from the various towns where they had been displayed and brought first to lie in state at the Palace of Holyrood, then borne in solemn procession up the same Royal Mile of Edinburgh where he had been sent to his death in a farm cart. He was buried in St. Giles Cathedral on 11 May 1661, while the bells of the city churches pealed and the guns of Edinburgh Castle boomed a salute.

His half-brother Harry rode, bearing the Montrose banner. James, now the Second Marquis of Montrose marched with his brother Robert behind the coffin, which was carried by fourteen Earls. Most of the great and good of Scotland duly fell into line, following Montrose's body in death when they had been too anxious for their own skins to follow him in life.

Argyll was not there to watch. Later that month, he was executed and his head placed on the Tolbooth spike so recently vacated by Montrose.

> **Being** defired to pray apart, He faid , I *have already powred out my foule before the Lord who knowes my heart , and into whofe hands I have commended my Spirit , and he hath been gratioufly pleafed to returne to me a full affurance of peace in Iefus Chrift my Redeemer. And therfore if you will not Ioine with me in prayer; my reiterating againe will be both Scandalous to you, and me.* So clofing his Eyes, & holding up his hands,he ftood a good fpace at his inward devotions , being perceived to be inwardly moved all the while; When He had don,He cald for the Executioner , & gave him money, then having brought unto him hanging in a cord His *Declaration,*& *Hiftorie ,* He hanged them about his necke;faying , *Though it hath pleafed His Sacred* MAJESTIE *that now is,to make him one of the Knights of the moft Honorable Order of the Garter; yet* He did not thinke him felfe more Honored by the Garter, then by that cord; *with the bookes which he would embrace about his neck with as much ioy & content, as ever he did the Garter, or a chaine of gould ,* & therfore defired them to be tied unto him as they pleafed.
> When this was done & His armes tied,He asked the Officers, *If they had any more Dishonour,as they conceaved it,to put upon him,he was readie to accept it.* And fo with an *Vndaunted Courage* & *Grayitie* suffered, According to the Sentence paft upon him.
>
> # FINIS.
>
> Anonymous contemporary eye-witness account of Montrose's death.

A BRIEF CHRONOLOGY

1612   Born, probably in October. Only son of John,
        Fourth Earl of Montrose and Margaret Ruthven,
        daughter of the Earl of Gowrie.

1626   Father dies at Kincardine Castle, Perthshire. James
        becomes Fifth Earl.

1627–29 Studies at St. Andrews University.

1629   Marries Magdalen Carnegie, daughter of Lord
        Kinnaird, later Earl of Southesk. They have five
        children: John (1630), James (1632), David (1639),
        and Robert and Jean (birth year unknown, but
        before 1642).

1633–36 Travels in France, Italy and Germany, despite Thirty
        Years War.

1636   Formally presented at London court of King
        Charles I.

1638   Signs The National Covenant, protesting against
        arbitrary royal appointments and interference in
        Scottish Presbyterian religion, but swearing
        allegiance to the king.

1639   Scotland fragments into civil war. Forced to choose
        between king and religious freedom, Montrose
        defeats royal anti-covenant troops at Brig o' Dee.

1640   Leads an army south to occupy Newcastle. King
        Charles I concedes to Scottish parliament the right
        to approve royal appointments.

1641   Scottish parliament, dominated by the Marquis
        of Argyll, becomes more extreme puritan and anti-
        monarchy. Montrose remains a moderate,
        preferring reform to revolution. He is imprisoned

for five months for failing to renounce the king. Covenanters ransack Kincardine Castle. Son David dies later.

1643   Montrose refuses to sign The Solemn League and Covenant, the manifesto of the Scottish Puritan extremists.

1644   King Charles I raises Montrose from an Earl to a Marquis and makes him Lieutenant Governor and Captain General of Scotland to defend the realm against Argyll's covenanting armies. Wins battles of Tippermuir, Aberdeen and Fyvie.

1645   Montrose invades Argyll's homeland and crushes his army at Inverlochy. Wins battles of Dundee, Auldearn, Alford and Kilsyth. His troops are depleted. Defeated at Philiphaugh by David Leslie's new professional covenanting army. Eldest son John dies. Second son, James imprisoned.

1646   Covenanters destroy Kincardine Castle. Wife Magdalen dies later. Younger children Robert and Jean rescued by Magdalen's father, Earl of Southesk. King Charles I captured by Puritans. Montrose driven into exile in Europe.

1646-49 Travels in war-torn Europe, trying to raise funds and troops to retake Scotland for the king. English royal courts in exile at Paris and at Breda in Holland are no help. Charles I is executed in London in 1649.

1650   New King Charles II, safe in Holland, persuades Montrose to return to Scotland. His small army is defeated at Carbisdale. Montrose is captured, taken to Edinburgh and executed without trial on 21 May 1650.

1660   Puritan extremist regime collapses. Charles II restores moderate royal rule.

1661   Montrose given a hero's funeral in Edinburgh on 11 May 1661.

BIBLIOGRAPHICAL NOTE ON MONTROSE'S POEMS

THERE ARE NO known contemporary manuscripts of Montrose's poems and we cannot tell how many of his poems have been lost. Those that survive may well contain corruptions of the original. Some of Montrose's papers were destroyed in 1641 when his enemies ransacked his houses in search of state secrets. Other documents have vanished since. Attribution is made more difficult by the fact that, as with some other major historical figures, like Mary, Queen of Scots, he has had poems ascribed to him that were instead the work of imitating admirers.

His poems have filtered down to us through the imperfect memories of loyal supporters and broadside balladeers. Fanciful stories have been added. The macabre Victorian antiquarian, J. W. Morkill who managed to purchase Montrose's right arm and sword, claimed that his *Metrical Vow* of vengeance for the death of Charles I was first written on Leith Sands with the point of that very sword. Montrose, however, received the news of Charles's death in the Netherlands, where he handed the poem to his chaplain, Wishart, three days later. His *Metrical Prayer Before Execution* is reputed to have been written with a diamond on his Tolbooth cell window. Montrose, however, almost certainly did have pen and paper that night whereas his cell window did not have glass.

The reality is more potent than the myth. Montrose has never been short of distinguished literary admirers. Drummond of Hawthornden wrote a moving poem *At the Funerals of Montrose*. Even Voltaire, in his *Essaie sur l'Histoire Generale*, praises both the nobility and the art of *His Metrical Prayer Before Execution*.

As far as we can tell, Montrose wrote poetry as an immediate, emotional response to great events rather than as carefully spun statements. Some of his poems have the flaws of writing at speed without revision. The best of them, however, have a power and dignity worthy of standing beside the best political writers of his age or any other.

I have tried to use the earliest credible source for each poem. For today's readers, who may care more about what he said than how various editors printed his words, I have standardised spelling and punctuation as far as reasonably possible. For those who wish to see the original texts, here are the main sources in chronological order. If anyone can find more of Montrose's poems, perhaps in a deed box in a Scottish house or among family memorabilia somewhere in Europe, I would be delighted.

George Wishart. *The History of the King's Majestie's Affaires in Scotland under the Conduct of the Most Honourable James, Marquess of Montrose, Earl of Kincardin etc and Governor of the Kingdome in the Years* 1644, 1645 *and* 1646. Published anonymously in Amsterdam. 1649.

The poem *Great! Good! And Just!* prefaces this book. It is the earliest copy of a poem by Montrose.

★ ★ ★

Montrose to His Mistress. A broadside from the library of Archibald Philip, Earl of Rosebery, now in the National Library of Scotland, bound in *Old Scotch Ballads and Broadsides* 1679-1730. Undated, but probably well before 1700.

Sadly, this is a poor version of the poem. It bears the hallmarks of the broadside balladeer who could not quite remember all the lines and had to improvise. The question of accuracy is complicated by the fact that Montrose based his poem upon a well-known popular song of the time. The verse order in Part II is different from other versions. I have not used it.

★ ★ ★

Henry Guthry, Bishop of Dunkeld. *Memoirs.* London. 1702.

Great! Good! And Just! is printed at the conclusion of the bishop's memoirs as an affirmation of his royalist sympathies.

★ ★ ★

James Watson. *A Choice Collection of Comic and Serious Scots Poems Both Ancient and Modern, By Several Hands. Part III.* Printed by James Watson and sold at his shop next door to the Red Lyon opposite to the Lucken-booths. Edinburgh. 1711.

We do not know exactly what sources Watson had, but his is an admirable collection, which has formed the basis of all subsequent editions of Montrose's poems. An edition of Watson, edited and excellently annotated by Harriet Harvey-Wood, published by The Scottish Text Society in 1991 is the handiest source for most scholars. Watson includes *To His Mistress, There's Nothing in this World Can Prove, In Praise of Women, On the Faithlessness and Venality of His Times, Burst Out My Soul in Main of Tears, Can Little Beasts with Lions Roar, Great! Good! And Just!* and *Let Them Bestow on Every Airth a Limb.* Watson also includes a poem, *The Tunnice [tennis] Court,* which has sometimes been ascribed to Montrose but whose rhythms of speech are so unlike his other works and whose sentiments are so meek and mild that it is hard to believe he wrote it. Watson's preface to Part I in 1706 ends 'the next collection shall consist wholly of poems never before printed, most of them being already in the undertaker's hands and shall (God Willing) be published at or before the First day of November next. In fact it took three more years for Part II and a further two for Part III. Publishers were ever thus.

★ ★ ★

James Maidment. *Scottish Pasquils* 1560-1715. Published 1827-28.

Maidment edited these pasquils from the papers of Sir James Balfour of Denmylne, Lord Lyon King of Arms under Charles II. It is the only known source for *Some Lynes on the Killing of ye Earle of Newcastell's Sonne's Dogge*. The collection also includes *Burst Out my Soul in Main of Tears* and, intriguingly, the *Pasquil on Argyll*.

The tone of the pasquil, the double meanings, biblical and classical allusions, are characteristic of Montrose and the last line anticipates his last words on the gallows, 'May God have mercy on this afflicted kingdom'. The sharp reply to the pasquil, with its snide logic and final dig at Graham, are aimed directly at Montrose. There is no hard evidence to attribute the original pasquil to Montrose, but it may be a corrupted version of a lost Montrose poem. I include it here for its historical interest and to point it out to future editors who may uncover sources that confirm or deny its attribution.

★ ★ ★

Robert Chambers. *History of the Rebellions in Scotland under the Marquis of Montrose and Others*. Edinburgh. 1828.

On page 324 of Vol II Chambers quotes the poem *I would be high, but that the cedar tree*, giving as his source a manuscript collection of Scottish poems and pasquils made at the end of the seventeenth century by David Gregory, Savilian Professor at Oxford.

★ ★ ★

Mark Napier. *Montrose and the Covenanters*. London. 1838.

Napier reprints the poems from Watson, plus the pasquil on the canicidal young Hamilton.

★ ★ ★

Mark Napier. *Memoirs of Montrose*. London. 1856.

To his credit, Napier discovered the poems written in the leaves of Montrose's books. He also discovered the Rosebery library broadsheet of *Montrose to his Mistress* or another copy of it, and concocted an awkward hybrid version between it and the Watson edition.

* * *

There are other lesser sources, but the most recent editions of Montrose's poems were edited, first by Robert Rait in 1901 who did no more than reprint the Watson poems, a feeble piece of scholarship for the principal of a university (Glasgow) and Historiographer Royal of Scotland and then in 1938 by J.L. Weir who says in his preface 'It seems most unlikely that any of his poems were published in his lifetime'. As we now know, Montrose went to the gallows with one of his printed poems hung round his neck.

I first edited *The Collected Poems of James Graham, First Marquis of Montrose* for an edition published by David Lewis, New York 1970. After further research, I compiled a new edition of *The Collected Poems of James Graham, First Marquis of Montrose* published in the UK by Mandeville Press 1990. Both of these books sold out quickly. Regrettably, second-hand copies are hard to find and very expensive. *Civil Warrior* is an attempt to make Montrose's poems available again and to give twenty-first-century readers some brief historical background to put his words in context.

TITLES AND FIRST LINES OF
MONTROSE'S POEMS

Some other books published by **LUATH** PRESS

HISTORY

Blind Harry's Wallace
William Hamilton of Gilbertfield
ISBN 0 946487 43 X HBK £15.00
ISBN 0 946487 33 2 PBK £8.99

The Quest for Arthur
Stuart McHardy
ISBN 1 84282 012 5 HBK £16.99

The Quest for the Celtic Key
Karen Ralls-Macleod
Ian Robertson
ISBN 0 946487 73 1 HBK £18.99

Reportage Scotland:
History in the Making
Louise Yeoman
Foreword by Professor David Stevenson
ISBN 0 946487 61 8 PBK £9.99

Old Scotland New Scotland
Jeff Fallow
ISBN 0 946487 40 5 PBK £6.99

SOCIAL HISTORY

A Word for Scotland
Jack Campbell
with a foreword by Magnus Magnusson
ISBN 0 946487 48 0 PBK £12.99

The Crofting Years
Francis Thompson
ISBN 0 946487 06 5 PBK £6.95

Shale Voices
Alistair Findlay
foreword by Tam Dalyell MP
ISBN 0 946487 63 4 PBK £10.99
ISBN 0 946487 78 2 HBK £17.99

TRAVEL & LEISURE

Let's Explore Edinburgh Old Town
Anne Bruce English
ISBN 0 946487 98 7 PBK £4.99

Edinburgh and Leith Pub Guide
Stuart McHardy
ISBN 0 946487 80 4 PBK £4.95

Edinburgh's Historic Mile
Duncan Priddle
ISBN 0 946487 97 9 PBK £2.99

Pilgrims In The Rough:
St Andrews beyond the 19th hole
Michael Tobert
ISBN 0 946487 74 X PBK £7.99

BIOGRAPHY

Bare Feet and Tackety Boots
Archie Cameron
ISBN 0 946487 17 0 PBK £7.95

Tobermory Teuchter: A first-hand
account of life on Mull in the early
years of the 20th century
Peter Macnab
ISBN 0 946487 41 3 PBK £7.99

Come Dungeons Dark
John Taylor Caldwell
ISBN 0 946487 19 7 PBK £6.95

The Last Lighthouse
Sharma Krauskopf
ISBN 0 946487 96 0 PBK £7.99

FICTION

The Road Dance
Sharma Krauskopf
ISBN 1 84282 024 9 PBK £9.99

The Bannockburn Years
William Scott
ISBN 0 946487 34 0 PBK £7.95

The Strange Case of R L Stevenson
Richard Woodhead
ISBN 0 946487 86 3 HBK £16.99

The Great Melnikov
Hugh Maclachlan
ISBN 0 946487 42 1 PBK £7.95

Grave Robbers
Robin Mitchell
ISBN 0 946487 72 3 PBK £7.95

But n Ben A-Go-Go
Matthew Fitt
ISBN 0 946487 82 0 HBK £10.99

CURRENT ISSUES

Trident on Trial
the case for people's disarmament
Angie Zelter
ISBN 1 84282 004 4 PBK £9.99

**Scotland - Land and Power
the agenda for land reform**
Andy Wightman
in association with
Democratic Left Scotland
foreword by Lesley Riddoch
ISBN 0 946487 70 7 PBK £5.00

Broomie Law
Cinders McLeod
ISBN 0 946487 99 5 PBK £4.00

NATURAL SCOTLAND

Wild Scotland: The essential guide to finding the best of natural Scotland
James McCarthy
Photography by Laurie Campbell
ISBN 0 946487 37 5 PBK £7.50

**Scotland Land and People
An Inhabited Solitude**
James McCarthy
ISBN 0 946487 57 X PBK £7.99

The Highland Geology Trail
John L Roberts
ISBN 0 946487 36 7 PBK £4.99

Rum: Nature's Island
Magnus Magnusson
ISBN 0 946487 32 4 PBK £7.95

Red Sky at Night
John Barrington
ISBN 0 946487 60 X PBK £8.99

Listen to the Trees
Don MacCaskill
ISBN 0 946487 65 0 PBK £9.99

Wildlife: Otters – On the Swirl of the Tide
Bridget MacCaskill
ISBN 0 946487 67 7 PBK £9.99

Wildlife: Foxes – The Blood is Wild
Bridget MacCaskill
ISBN 0 946487 71 5 PBK £9.99

POETRY

Poems to be read aloud
Collected and with an introduction by
Tom Atkinson
ISBN 0 946487 00 6 PBK £5.00

Scots Poems to be read aloud
Collected and with an introduction by
Stuart McHardy
ISBN 0 946487 81 2 PBK £5.00

The Luath Burns Companion
John Cairney
ISBN 1 84282 000 1 PBK £10.00

Men & Beasts
Poems and Prose by Valerie Gillies
Photographs by Rebecca Marr
ISBN 0 946487 92 8 PBK £15.00

'Nothing but Heather!'
Gerry Cambridge
ISBN 0 946487 49 9 PBK £15.00

SPORT

Over the Top with the Tartan Army (Active Service 1992-97)
Andrew McArthur
ISBN 0 946487 45 6 PBK £7.99

MUSIC AND DANCE

Highland Balls and Village Halls
GW Lockhart
ISBN 0 946487 12 X PBK £6.95

Fiddles & Folk
GW Lockhart
ISBN 0 946487 38 3 PBK £7.95

NEW SCOTLAND

**Notes from the North
incorporating a Brief History of the Scots and the English**
Emma Wood
ISBN 0 946487 46 4 PBK £8.99

Luath Press Limited
committed to publishing well written books worth reading

LUATH PRESS takes its name from Robert Burns, whose little collie Luath (*Gael.*, swift or nimble) tripped up Jean Armour at a wedding and gave him the chance to speak to the woman who was to be his wife and the abiding love of his life. Burns called one of *The Twa Dogs* Luath after Cuchullin's hunting dog in *Ossian's Fingal*. Luath Press grew up in the heart of Burns country, and now resides a few steps up the road from Burns' first lodgings in Edinburgh's Royal Mile. Luath offers you distinctive writing with a hint of unexpected pleasures.

Most UK and US bookshops either carry our books in stock or can order them for you. To order direct from us, please send a £sterling cheque, postal order, international money order or your credit card details (number, address of cardholder and expiry date) to us at the address below. Please add post and packing as follows: UK – £1.00 per delivery address; overseas surface mail – £2.50 per delivery address; overseas airmail – £3.50 for the first book to each delivery address, plus £1.00 for each additional book by airmail to the same address. If your order is a gift, we will happily enclose your card or message at no extra charge.

Luath Press Limited
543/2 Castlehill
The Royal Mile
Edinburgh EH1 2ND
Scotland
Telephone: 0131 225 4326 (24 hours)
Fax: 0131 225 4324
email: gavin.macdougall@luath.co.uk
Website: www.luath.co.uk